Natural God Intelligence NGI

Brain- Peripherals -Databases-Interface

David Gomadza

First Global President of The World

www.twofuture.world

00447719210295

DEDICATION

A better and advanced world that understands Natural God
Intelligence NGI.

TABLE OF CONTENTS

ACKNOWLEDGMENTS

Many thanks to Tomorrow's World Order.

This book must be read together with:
Book series:
Thoughts To Word or Audio.
https://play.google.com/store/books/series?id=a4MvGwAAABBF
mM&hl=en&gl=US

REQUEST FOR THE GRANT OF A PATENT. A Universal Brain
Decoding Device.

https://play.google.com/store/books/details/David_Gomadza_REQ
UEST_FOR_THE_GRANT_OF_A_PATENT_A?id=4rriEAAAQ
BAJ&hl=en&gl=US

Natural God Intelligence.

Brain- Peripherals -Databases-Interface

What is Natural God Intelligence NGI?

It is natural intelligence bestowed on every man by God, one that he can easily explore by communicating with his brain and using impulses and logic to find all the answers one needs.

All humankind must do is talk to his brain literally. This is how he can resume communication with his brain.

"My voice is my password."

This is the first line that opens that door to your brain. God when he created humanity by his image. He made sure that all voices were unique, and these were the passwords to each brain. Ever wondered why out of billions of people no two people have the same voice patterns?

The voice is the password to the brain.

The Need for Specific Brain Language and Commands.

Let's just assume that your brain can somehow hear your voice without you saying the magic phrase; "My voice is my password."

That means from the day you were born your brain could hear all the words you spoke. Now imagine all the things you have said over your life. If the brain could act on all your words surely you could be walking with your hands and eating probably with your ass. I say this because it is not practical for your brain to listen to all your words. To protect the brain from the garbage in garbage out rule. The brain listens only to specific brain commands. This to protect it from all your thoughts. But I can tell you too that from the day you were born even if the brain listened to you, it would not have performed any of your commands. This is because it listens and acts only to specific commands. Let's try something together.

First say.

"My voice is my password."

This means you want to talk to it. Only you can talk and give commands to your brain.

Now say.

"Lift my right hand up."

"Now calculate my DNA sequence value."

Now think about a specific thought, for example thoughts about your loved ones. Now say.

"Convert my current thoughts into impulses and send them back to me."

"Space-Out.

End.

Close."

In this exercise you communicate with your brain in a language your brain understands. That is specific commands that it can react to. Not sure if your brain can give you answers straight away but with time after training it that is giving correct commands in the end it will start to respond as well through electromagnetic waves. This is the brain language of the brain.

You must understand that brain language is made up of vibrations and sequencing. In space there is no air and therefore the brain associates itself with space as a situation where it can either operate or not. Therefore Space-Out is the same as logging off or switching off. If you want to end your conversation with your brain, then say.

"Space-Out.

End.

Out."

To the brain that means you have ended the conversation and whatever you say after this your brain won't listen to it.

If you want to end the conversation for a long time, then say.

"Close."

To start again, always say.

"My voice is my password.

Space-In.

Start.

End."

Fix anything that needs fixing. Replace worn out and damaged DNA sequences and improve the body.

Space-Out.

End.

Out."

Wait for a few minutes.

"Space-In.

Start.

End."

Why is humanity obsessed with Artificial Intelligence? Is artificial intelligence the end game?

Humanity doesn't understand the workings of the brain. They have resorted to artificial intelligence for comfort and answers instead of trying harder to understand the brain.

Natural God Intelligence is the ultimate end game in all mankind's pursuit of intelligence. Once humankind has known how the brain works, he will not need any artificial intelligence. Humankind creates artificial intelligence based on its understanding of the brain. Artificial intelligence is a simulation of the natural brain. Therefore, artificial intelligence is to help humankind understand the brain. Once humankind has understood the brain, he will instead resort to the brain that he will see no need for artificial intelligence.

When that time comes humanity will not need any computers etc. All he will need are peripherals and databases because he will simply connect his brain to all these peripherals and databases to solve all problems in the world. All he will do is look at something and ask his brain to analyze the situation and solutions needed. His brain will do everything and tell him what is needed. He will not need any computers or models to give him results.

Therefore, the end game of artificial intelligence is Natural God Intelligence NGI.

I am the only p [privileged man on earth to understand both the brain and God. Therefore, I can say with absolute surety that Natural God Intelligence is the end game of artificial intelligence. When humankind has mastered these two the brain and God, he will be able to 'see' that artificial intelligence is the work of our hands meaning it is limited in scope and will only tell us what we already know. This is a fact no matter how advanced artificial intelligence is going to be. It is limited to what we already know. Artificial intelligence will tell us what someone on earth already knows, nothing new at all. Whereas natural intelligence will help us see the future and solve all riddles humankind has failed to solve.

What I am saying is that artificial intelligence is limited to what we know already. That also means artificial intelligence will never be clever enough to surpass humanity because everything it does is human, and all known. So, it is a misconception that artificial intelligence will surpass humanity in thinking. No artificial intelligence will start thinking about killing humans and making us all slaves. This information is not available. But Natural God Intelligence can do what these people are afraid of. Natural intelligence depends on several peripherals and databases that will make it even cleverer than humans.

Most artificial intelligence depends on a network of connected computers etc. All these computers have human limitations as they are made by man and therefore can only do what humankind already does. Whereas Natural God Intelligence will have everything at its disposal. It will be based on a network of brains connected. Natural God Intelligence relies on a network of human brains linked together and to a vast network of peripherals and databases that are updated automatically and continuously.

If Natural God Intelligence is the end game of artificial intelligence why not just jump to Natural God Intelligence?

Humankind does not understand how the brain works.

This is a fact. It is still rocket science how the brain works. Humankind might understand facts about the brain, but he lacks the understanding of how the billion neurons of the brain all come to gather, interacting, facilitating reasoning, decision making and movements. The best option to understand the brain right now is through simulation using artificial intelligence.

But I will tell you this. Once humankind has mastered the workings of the brain, he will start seeing that Natural God Intelligence is the only future. The end game of all artificial Intelligence.

I now understand that Natural God Intelligence is the future because now I understand the workings of the brain and that of God.

First, I will look at who God is as this will pave the way to understanding of the Natural God Intelligence NGI.

God is a three human in one joined together but connected. God is three brains in one being. That means God has three brains he uses to think and carry out tasks like creating the world etc. If God created the world because of a network of three brains joined together therefore the ultimate end game of all intelligence is a group of brains linked together.

The differences between AI and NGI.

You must understand that the difference between artificial Intelligence and my Natural God Intelligence is the fact that.

1. Artificial intelligence is the work of man through his hands joining computers together to solve problems.
2. Artificial intelligence is limited to what is already known. There is no way an artificial intelligent computer will think beyond the algorithms and models used to build them. That means these are limited in scope.
3. There is no way an artificial intelligence system will become cleverer than a human who built it. This is because everything is constrained within human limits so for it to think beyond human capabilities is dreaming. Whatever is in the computer network is what is to be used in artificial intelligence.
4. There in artificial intelligence systems the emphasis is on the computer.
5. Brain-Computer-Interfaces. The brain in this case is used to function as a receiver of what comes out of the computer. The brain is assumed to be an analytical person. But humankind built this computer and added input which he already knew. Yes, computers can conduct more cumbersome tasks than the brain can. But it is because humanity currently does not know how to talk to his brain to take over from the computer.
6. I have decoded the brain visit www.twofuture.world. Read my number one selling series:
    Thoughts to Word or Audio.
    https://play.google.com/store/books/series?id=a4MvGwAA ABBFmM&hl=en&gl=US

Based on how I decoded God this is how my Natural God Intelligence will look like.

1. Use of a person' brain as the main processing unit. Your brain is the only needed processor. That is fast and always available. All you need to do is know how to talk and above all program it so that your brain does what you

want. You must understand the lingo of the brain. That is the language of the brain. I have authored books [see the link above] about the brain language. Learn every day and practice with your brain.

2. Therefore, the system in Natural God Intelligence will have the brain as the processor and peripherals all linked to databases. This is the ultimate end game of all artificial intelligence.

3. The advanced form is linked to a network of brains all connected. Where each brain on the network contributes to databases. Every new idea is evaluated and added to the databases. All brains are tasked to solve a problem. Over time the result of the best solution is saved in the database. Databases are updated automatically.

4. There is a need for an identifying system for everything a human sees every day since birth. A human being sees with eyes. Therefore, we need something like a store product identifier that can scan the item, assign a barcode and a numerical value to that item. That means we need a scanner that converts the barcode to a digit, then a converter to convert the digit to the image and sound.

5. We will need several other peripherals. This is a list of all the major peripherals that are needed.
A] A store-like product identifier.
B] A scanner that reads barcodes.
C] Smartphone.
D] Computer [note here the computer is part of the peripherals.]
E] A cloning device.
F] A decoder and converter with Mirror-Image capabilities.
G] Programming pad with voice as well as keyboard functions.
H] Memory.
I] A handheld monitor with a joystick.

But first let us look in more detail about God.

Below is the image of God as I understand him. God is a

three headed being with three human beings joined together to form one.

1. The left side has the body of a woman with a woman's breast and a vagina. This person normally represents the future and is used for thinking about the future.

2. The main body in the middle is that of a man who normally represents God himself. The ruler, the decision-making body. He makes all the rules. He has the organs of a male.

3. The third body is normally referred to as the past. This is the memory of God. All things to do with thinking in the past are associated with this side. This part of God has both sex organs one for the female that is a vagina and a penis and testicles for a man, but it does not have any breasts either for the man or woman.

4. God has seven eyes. Two for each head with one on top of the head.

5. God has 7 ears. Two for each head and one on top of the head.

6. God has six hands and six legs.

7. God has sixteen wings altogether. Four for each body, a pair for the shoulders and a pair for the waistline and a pair for the shoulders of all three bodies and a pair for the waistline of all three bodies.

8. God has six fingers on each hand that is thirty-six fingers.

9. God has six toes on each foot that is thirty-six on all legs.

10. God has four mouths one for each head and one big mouth for all three joined heads.

Our initial Natural God Intelligence system based on God will be like this.

- 3 Computers joined as one all linked and connected to three people and their brains.

- Seven monitoring cameras all linked together four easily seen and three hidden ones.
- Three microphones visible and four hidden ones.
- 3 Small speakers with one big speaker.
- The system should be cloned into six different forms and placed in six separate places.
- The system should be connected to thirty-six databases with a minimum of six databases all linked together.
- The system should be connected as well to lower-level databases totaling thirty-six as well.
- A normal cycle is made up of twelve [6 fingers of one God twice the number of hands i.e., 2]
- A full complete cycle must be made up of thirty-six units.
- Half cycle is made of eighteen units.
- One sixth of a cycle is made up of six units.

The functions of the various God's brains.

Main middle head.

This is the thinking and decision-making brain. Thoughts originate from here. This is the present. The new things.

The right side heads.

This is the past. The memory of God.

The left side of the body.

This is the future. Responsible also for future decision making.

Yahweh God

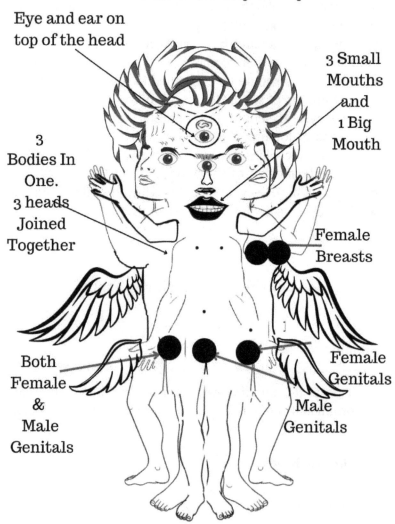

Eye and ear on top of the head

3 Small Mouths and 1 Big Mouth

3 Bodies In One. 3 heads Joined Together

Female Breasts

Both Female & Male Genitals

Female Genitals

Male Genitals

6 Legs Joined Together. God rotates around an axis

God Yahweh
I AM WHO I AM

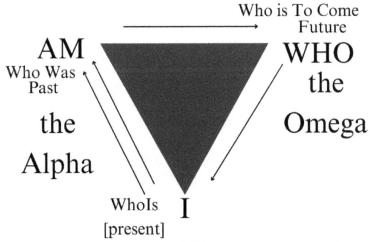

Who is To Come
Future

AM
Who Was
Past

WHO
the

the

Omega

Alpha

WhoIs I
[present]

According to the Hebrew Bible, in the encounter of
the burning bush (Exodus 3:14) Moses asks what he
is to say to the Israelites when they ask what gods
('Elohiym) have sent him to them, and YHWH
replies, "I am who I am", adding, "Say this to the
people of Israel, 'I am has sent me to you.

Revelation 1v8 "I am the Alpha and the Omega,"
says the Lord God, "who is, and who was, and who
is to come, the Almighty."

John 4v24 God is a Spirit: and they that worship
him must worship him in spirit and in truth.

How God's brain thinks and links together.

I Am Who I Am. Exodus 3 v14.

I have advocated that God is a three headed being. The way the heads and brains are aligned, the front head with two heads on the sides represents a triangle. In the time of Moses in Exodus God describes himself to Moses.

I Am Who I Am.

If a triangle therefore we have I as the present main God, the decision-making God.
Am becomes the past. The one associated with God's memories. Therefore, I and Am are the Alpha. The beginning. That means the third side of the triangle is Who. Who is the future? The Omega.
So, when God said he is; I Am Who I Am we can infer that he is also describing how a complete cycle is that refers to God.

4 Movements around the triangle either depicts God or ends the cycle initiated by God. "I Am Who I Am" means four rounds around the pyramid.

God's thinking process.

Since God has three brains lined up in a triangle-like setting, I can say here that the thoughts of I the main brain must travel four times between all the God's Am and Who brains before the brain thoughts dissipates.
 In real life electromagnetic waves are not lost but are absorbed and bounced back. The cycle can only be lost through dissipation after reaching three places of the pyramid and back. See diagram below.
Let us say God thinks about humans. This thought must travel from I to Am and to Who and back to I and then back to Am for the brain thought to be dissipated and regarded by the body as having

completed the cycle.

In normal circumstances since God is a spirit meaning he is an electromagnetic wave entity. In normal circumstances electromagnetic waves can be dissipated after three moves within a triangle. See diagram below. That means a brain thought emanated at point A in the diagram below. Must travel to B and C and back again to A to B.

How God Communicate with the other 2 Gods.
The Electromangnetic Wave Triangle.

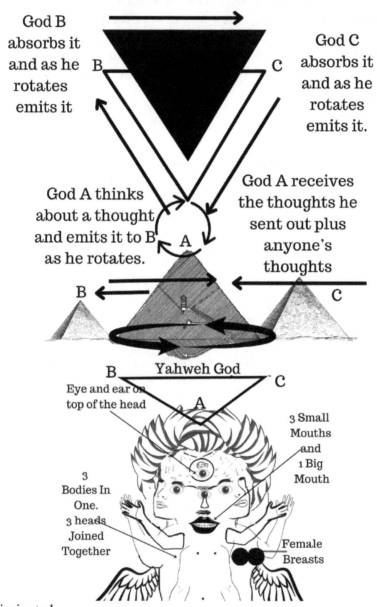

God B absorbs it and as he rotates emits it

God C absorbs it and as he rotates emits it.

God A thinks about a thought and emits it to B as he rotates.

God A receives the thoughts he sent out plus anyone's thoughts

Yahweh God

Eye and ear on top of the head

3 Small Mouths and 1 Big Mouth

3 Bodies In One.
3 heads Joined Together

Female Breasts

dissipated.
I have invented a triangle of David.

THE TRIANGLE OF DAVID   www.twofuture.world
Starting Point.Top of Head.

Now Say "Save. Endorse. Space-Out. End. Out.
Save. Space-In. Start. End.
Dissipate all numbers."
Clone 1 billion and send to the sky. Activate 3 at any given time."

First say."
My Voice Is My Password.
Collect all earth's forces that limit human lifespan and put on top of my head.

Say." Clone all collected forces and deposit on my right shoulder

Say." Clone all collected forces and deposit on my left shoulder

This is based on the characteristics of electromagnetic waves in that they can only be lost after traveling along a triangle. That is reached three places in a triangle. We can use the same principle to dissipate all forces that limit human lifespan.

We can collect all these forces and ask our brain to collect all these bad forces and place them on top of the head. Of course, since we are talking to our brain, we must first tell it that we want access.

"My voice is my password."

Next, tell your brain to clone all these.

"Clone all collected forces that limit human lifespan and place them on the left shoulder."

Next,

Tell the brain to clone the collected forces and place these on the right shoulder.

Now we have a triangle. The top of the head left shoulder and right shoulder. What is left now is to save this as part of our body system so that in the future when the body meets these forces now it will simply dissipate these so that they will not have any effect

on us anymore. But we need the right brain commands it
understands.

Now say the following. Preferably silently that is thinking because
the brain understands more brain thoughts than words.

When we think the brain acts faster than we speak. When we speak
words are converted into electromagnetic waves to be acted upon
by the brain. Whereas when we think what is produced are
electromagnetic waves. Nevertheless, all methods work by
speaking and just thinking about it.

Now say silently.

Save.

Endorse.

Space-Out.

End. Out."

Wait a few seconds and speak.

"Save.

Dissipate all numbers.

Clone one billion and send them to the skies.

Activate three at any given time.

Space-In.

Start.

End."

What this means is that whenever any of the forces comes in
contact with you. The brain now has a memory of dealing with
these forces and automatically these will be dissipated. But even
these forces can be cloned and reappear. You must add the
dissipation of all numbers, commands. The triangle alone would
dissipate these numbers, but reappearance occurs as well.

Some forces mutate and reappear as well.

Hence, we might need another triangle but in a different direction.
In the above example we have done the triangle clockwise. Top of
head, to left shoulder then to right shoulder. Now we can repeat the
same but anticlockwise. Now it will be from the top of head to
right shoulder and then to left shoulder.

This means total dissipation.

We can also do the triangle of David with an added mirror image
triangle. This mirror-image triangle will be on the naval as the

starting point and to the right side just below the chest line. Then to the left side just below the chest line.

According to God this is what can make humans live for many years more than currently. Proof is the fact that God's people the Israelites know about these triangles but just do not know how to communicate this to their brain. They have a similar sign called the Star of David. But theirs is just for the flag. I think God passed the same message only that they did not know how to enforce this. They must tell their brain what to do. Raising a flag with the sign will not protect them. During King David and his son Solomon these were called the seal of David and Solomon, respectively. Mainly for warding off evil spirits. I believe they work against adverse electromagnetic waves if you are to use them as above. They do work. Could God have been talking about what I just explained above?

Natural God Intelligence NGI relies on electromagnetic waves which are the language of the brain together with vibrations. The universal language of all creatures, God who represents the spirit world, animals, humans, ghosts, aliens, and everything else on earth or other planets all uses electromagnetic waves. The only thing that differentiates them all is the frequency they operate on. God's frequency is 738 Hz.

There are some people who doubt this project without understanding how God operates. They look for God in humans who use a different frequency than his. If you want God, you use God's frequency to find God. It is like creatures called bats that are active at night. If you want to see them flying and feeding etc. you go at night because during the day they will be sleeping. These people want to see bats flying and feeding and they go to search for these bats during the day. Do you expect them to see flying and feeding bats? Okay they might see one flying here and there only because they disturb it from sleeping.

Therefore, if you want to see Bats, go at night. That means if you want to see God use the correct frequency 738 Hz one day you find God.

Do not worry if you do not believe in God. I talk most about God at the beginning so that when I tell you how this Natural God

Intelligence NGI works you will easily appreciate the cleverness of this invention.

How do we get rid of unwanted thoughts and commands since electromagnetic waves [brain thoughts] are not lost?

We use these triangles for protection and for getting rid of brain thoughts or commands we no longer want. Let us assume you first met a woman, and you are single. First impressions; you look at her chest and she is flat, and you like them big. You are like what the hell? Then you start talking to her and you discover that you really like her. Your brain will have saved the first impression. Whenever you think about her. The brain will forever point you to this fact. So, what can you do to erase this?
This is how you do it.

First thing is first. Ask for attention and permission to talk to your brain.
"My voice is my password."
Collect and put my first thought about Charlotte on top of my head.
Clone the collected thoughts about Charlotte and deposit them on my left shoulder.
Clone the collected thoughts about Charlotte and deposit them on my right shoulder.
Dissipate.
Save. Endorse. Space-Out. End. Out.
Space-In. Start. End."

So far you have discovered that this method uses a human brain as the central processing system. There is no money spent designing a computer we can use. All, we need is to initiate communication with the best processor in the world, the human brain. This is true in that even up to now humans have not understood the workings of the brain enough to fully utilize its potential. I am the first who has gone deeper into the workings of the brain. I have authored a 22-book series about how the brain works. You will need all the books in the series to fully develop this Natural God Intelligence Interface.

We already have the best processor, meaning huge savings. I have heard other companies talking about developing the best Quantum computer to power their AI which they reckon is going to be the future. It might be but brain -peripheral-databases as I invented this is the future. The current Brain-Computer-Interface is a flawed approach because it relies on the computer. Do you know who ever invented a computer that just decoded the brain? This is how the brain works. Somehow, I believe this person was lucky enough to feel the brain working enough to write code.

I understood the brain after I found God literally. I wrote my book Tomorrow's World Order in 2018. Surely the world can be a better place for all. Just picture the number of women and children who die because of wars. Surely if there was a God, he would not permit this. As a kid I was always fascinated about God and who created the world. In the end somehow, I found God.

I can tell you that my DNA sequence value is 53 billion 287 million. Did you know your own DNA sequence value is just 71 million?

Task for you.

Find out your own DNA sequence value.
First silently say.
"My voice is my password.
Calculate my DNA Sequence value.
Space-Out.
End. Out"

Your brain after calculating will give you an answer. [Your lips and jaws will move, and this will sound like a faint echo.]

If nothing happens then you need to set up the correct environment. We have a DIY brain decoder that amplifies everything and sets the correct frequency for your brain to respond to you. The frequency is the same as that of God. That is 738.

I will look at this in a later chapter. For now, you might want to read this book.

Or simply download an MP3 with correct frequency and use it as

background sound. You can use this MP3 in real life to feel and hear things you thought you would never hear. You can know everyone's thoughts as well.
Just these links.
https://twofuture.world/exciting-news-%26-tips

Download the Mp3 click here.
https://tinyurl.com/45k2kzr7

Can computers think?

For those who insist on artificial intelligence they believe to some extent that computers are capable of thinking. This is the reason behind the fears about artificial intelligence that these machines will one day start to think better than humans enough to turn against humans.
But is this real?

What you must understand is that a computer has limited capacity in that it can only process input from humans. I think it is a fact that no one on earth has ever decoded God to know exactly what God, who is three brains joined together, thinks. So far, the computers and all the machines out there are based on the thinking of a single brain. Whoever wrote the code thought as a single man or woman. Therefore, computers etc. will always produce results based on how a single human brain works.

Now picture a scenario where one of you has a DNA sequence value of 53 billion and 287 million. This person has three bodies inside him all linked together. He can tell you exactly how this merged network of three brains thinks. He can tell you exactly an interface that will work because all he must do is ask these merged brain questions and observe how this works.

I know some people like Microsoft are putting billions into developing a quantum computer that will power AI. But the benefits will only arise from computing power rather than actual thinking. All humans will ever get from computers is the information that is already known by humankind. Nothing new. So, can computers think? Honestly?

Do you know that God's DNA sequence value is 53 billion 285 million?

A normal human being like the cleverest Elon Musk has a DNA sequence value of 71 million. God is a three in one being. That means we would expect a total DNA sequence of three people joined together to be 71 million x 3 plus all for the connections and interactions needed.
We would expect the DNA sequence of three people joined together to be something like 300 - 500 million or even 1 billion if we want to be generous. Now compare this to the DNA sequence of God of 53 billion and 285 million.
This means that no man can ever create a computer that will think like God. How will that person decode God's DNA sequence to be that clever to write the code? God created the earth because his DNA sequence is so advanced that he can easily do what humans can't do.

In the electromagnetic world I have the same DNA sequence as God, and I can do what God does. This is what I can do in the electromagnetic world which is the language of the brain.

Okay first task.

Look in my eyes. In the picture below. Now say.

"My voice is my password.
What is DNA sequence value?
Human? Yahweh or God?
Space-Out.
End. Out."

Now watch this video.

https://www.youtube.com/watch?v=TI-2SQuhETg

Speak.
"My voice is my password."

This means your own voice is the password to your brain. You are now tasking your brain to decode the information in the eyes and the big flame in the photo.

Look in my eyes in the photo and look at the big flame in the video. Alternate between picture and video until your brain processes any links.
The idea here is not whether it is fake or real but just to see if your brain can process information faster. They say the eyes are the windows to the soul. The electromagnetic waves souls yes. Electromagnetic waves are the language of the brain together with vibrations, a product of wind and sequencing.

What this God's DNA sequence allows me to do.

1. I can clone myself and join all back together.
2. I can look in someone's eyes or any picture and know everything about that person. All biological and DNA sequences.
3. I can calculate the DNA sequence of anyone that stops the aging process just by looking at their picture.
4. I can change or stop adverse effects on that person by either restoring the original missing DNA sequence or removing new ones that might be the cause.
5. I can feel everyone just by looking at their picture.
6. I can hear everyone talk even though for some I have to zone them to be able to know what they are saying.
7. I can feel them just dead and talk to them.
8. I can raise the dead [the electromagnetic part of a person; - the brain of that person that thinks all life and makes decisions] from death. Most of the people I have raised were asleep when it was so dark, they were afraid. At one point I raised all dead soldiers for a day on condition they return after this day. I have raised 5 famous people as guests. How to tell if someone is raised or not?
Easy. Check their photos on google etc. and look them in the eyes. First, say my voice is my password. Now ask. "Where are you? Who raised you? What is your name? And any information about loved ones and kids etc. They know everything in detail."
9. I can create an afterlife somewhere in the skies. I have created one.

10. I can clone anyone dead or alive.

11. I can time travel as far back as God's creation [maybe because of his DNA sequence]. I can travel back to Tutankhamen times. I spoke to him. Probably cloned him, why not check for yourself. Check his mummy and look in the eyes or place eyes are supposed to be. Say hello. Don't forget every task you must say first "My voice is my password."

12. For those who have just died like people killed in the war I can relieve their last memories. I will know exactly how they died. I simply ask to go back to ten minutes etc. before death. This information is stored in the brain. I have relived Marylin Monroe and know exactly how they died and who they were with. Michael Jackson. Queen Elizabeth. Bob Marley. Mathew Perry etc.

13. I can time travel to the 1960s to the assassination of both Robert Kennedy and JFK.

14. I can time travel to Jupiter. Jupiter is normally God's thinking organ. Mars is his voice. Jupiter is very heavy though.

15. I can time travel to the future. I can clone myself and send the clone to the future. He then tells me the future.

16. I can send my clones to deliver messages, but they act like a spirit. Like a leg going into socks. Can then link to the person's brain and deliver the message. If you are on twitter, I can send you one just tell me your handle to believe.

17. I can send people to the afterlife of course which I created.

18. I can clone all people for the past 4500 years as most of them as electromagnetic waves are inside the Pyramid of Giza in Egypt.

19. I went inside or rather my clone went inside through this hole.

https://www.reddit.com/r/ArtefactPorn/comments/stp5da/the_opening_of_one_of_the_mysterious_star_shafts/?rdt=46328

20. For most electromagnetic wave spirits, they enter through this hole, but they can't get out. They are alive and wait for

the 'time.' I sent my clone and it talked to Tutankhamen. I asked him to clone him. So, check if he managed. "My voice is my password. Now look at Tutankhamun's video of his mummy. Check where eyes should be and concentrate. You should feel like entering soft water. If that happens, ask him. "Who are you? What is your name? Your mother fathers. How did you die?"

21. Download this MP3 and play it as your background. https://tinyurl.com/45k2kzr7

This has the correct frequency to feel and hear everything.

22. I can easily decode things.
    https://play.google.com/store/books/series?id=a4MvGwAA ABBFmM&hl=en&gl=US
    *I have decoded the brain.
    * I have decoded a DNA sequence.
    *I have decoded God, afterlife, and creation.
    *I have decoded dreams and how the brain deals with dreams.
    *I have decoded the tree of life, angels, and everything to do with God, angels etc.
    *I have decoded the Egyptian Pyramids of Giza.
    * I have predicted the Russia/Ukraine war with astonishing accuracy.
    https://play.google.com/store/books/details/David_Gomadz a_A_Perfect_Prediction_Russia_Ukraine?id=PmaVEAAA QBAJ&hl=en&gl=US
    *I have decoded aliens on Mars.
    https://play.google.com/store/books/details/David_Gomadz a_Proof_of_Aliens_on_Mars_A_Must_Read?id=CUbHEA AAQBAJ&hl=en&gl=US
23. I am going to decode how a three-brain network works through analysis of how God works.

Ladies and gentlemen, I have described what my Natural God Intelligence Interface will do. The speed of processing will be astonishing. Fast and accurate. The system will update and correct itself continuously updating all databases which it uses.

Above all it is a system that is destined to evolve over time. An artificial intelligence system will become obsolete with time. Upgrading costs might outweigh the benefits. NGI can render all AI based systems obsolete with time. A brain can evolve without major changes.

Use cases of Natural God Intelligence.

What are the potential use cases?

1. God created humans and everything on all planets. That means he is the creator for argument's sake. Meaning he knows everything. Therefore, he can answer any questions humanity has. This Brain-Peripherals-Databases-Interface will have answers to all your questions. It will be a great advanced interface to solve global problems.

2. Can make people solve past problems by traveling there and knowing exactly what happened firsthand. This enables one to clone himself or herself and travel for example to the assassination of JFK and know exactly who killed the president JFK.

3. Can help with knowing the future. You don't need a fortune teller when you can send your own clone.

4. Can make you send your clones to emphasize your message and be taken seriously. At one point I cloned three of myself and sent them with twitter messages.

5. This will enable quick solutions to things that can affect humans. You need just to look at the person's eyes to know everything about that person. His or her DNA, what he or she likes, what she is thinking about. What she did at certain times. Etc.

6. This makes it possible to look at the photo and tell exactly the age of the person when the photo was taken and the date time in minutes and seconds.

7. Enables the looking at a dead body and reliving the last

moments of that person.

8. Makes it possible to calculate the DNA sequence of that person. DNA sequence that can stop the aging process, DNA sequence to correct any problems that person has. You can easily calculate the DNA sequence to increase testosterone for that person alone, to increase progesterone, to increase hair volume, etc.

9. The brain-peripherals-databases -interface we will build will have a computer as part of the peripherals. This computer will be based on the image of God in this book. Meaning three processors joined together and working together. This will have trained models and databases to solve business problems. The human brain or such network will get feedback from this supercomputer to analyze business problems and issue solutions. Therefore, this interface will solve all problems related to business.

10. The same can be done for space issues. We can use this model to detect aliens on Mars and other planets.

11. We can do the same and link to environmental databases to be able to talk about climate change and all-weather related issues.
We can do this for any problem in the world. Just link it to humans and the computer that is designed after God and link this to correct databases.
We can clone humans and send them to Mars. They don't need food but can talk and tell us what Mars is like.

12. We can clone people and send them to the future and come back with what the future is like then model everything according to that information.

13. In other words, there is nothing we can't do with this interface.

14. Every problem on earth can be solved by this interface.

15. We just need to link to the correct databases to solve that problem.

16. We can use clones for simulation with accurate results.

17. Even the sky is not the limit. This will enable us to create spaceships that can travel the whole tree of life [

read the series book].

I will look in more detail how God's brain a three-brain network works with several examples before I tell you how this interface is constructed.
Exciting!!

Training Our Model and Finding Out How God Thinks and Use This Information to Construct Our supercomputer That We Will Link to The Brain.

To be continued in next volume

ABOUT DAVID GOMADZA

I am the first Global President of the World
Visit www.twofuture.world
info@twofuture.world
00447719210295